# SAMPLE PROBLEMS FROM THE STEVENS MATH OLYMPIADS

1. Sample problems

Below are three sample problems per division of the Stevens Math Olympiad, held annually at Stevens Institute of Technology in Hoboken, New Jersey. The sample problems are taken from the Olympiads held in 2016, 2017, and 2018. Answers are given on the last page.

Note that Olympiad problems are intended to be challenging! Challenging problems both contribute to the spirit of a mathematics competition and help us single out winners from a large pool of participants. Solving even a handful of problems at the Olympiad (each student will be offered 15 problems) is a result to be proud of.

### Grades 3-4

(1) An ant travels around a circle in the direction shown. As it moves, it touches each of the labeled points in order. The first three points that the ant touches are $A$, $B$, and $C$, in that order. What is the 28th point that the ant touches?

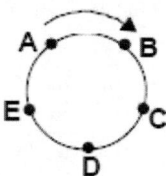

(2) Camila is hanging upside-down from the monkey bars at the playground. If her left ear is facing east, then what direction is her nose facing?

(3) A rectangle has a perimeter of 2 meters and a length of 70 centimeters. Find the area of the rectangle in square centimeters.

### Grades 5-6

(1) Nicole has three times as many stickers as Sharon. Sharon has twice as many stickers as Ariel. If Ariel has fewer than 8 stickers, then what is the greatest number of stickers that Nicole can have?

(2) The denominators of two fractions are consecutive natural numbers. Both fractions are in lowest terms, and their sum is $\dfrac{51}{56}$. Find the greater of the two fractions.

(3) When a four-digit number is divided by 3 or by 7, the remainder is 1. A Stevens professor doubles this number, then writes the result on a whiteboard. What is the smallest possible value of the number written by the professor?

## Grades 7-8

(1) Each of 25 cards is labeled either with the number 3 or 4. The sum of all of the numbers on the cards is 88. How many cards are labeled with the number 3?

(2) In the addition problem

$$\text{STEVENS} + \text{HOBOKEN} = 9495753,$$

each letter stands for one of the digits $0, 1, \ldots, 9$. The same letter always stands for the same digit, and different letters stand for different digits. Assuming the addition is correct, what four-digit number does the word HENS represent?

(3) A particle is located at vertex $A$ of the triangle $ABC$ shown below. Suppose that the particle randomly takes a step along one of the edges of the triangle, with equal probability assigned to each adjacent vertex. What is the probability that the particle will first return to vertex $A$ after 5 or more steps?

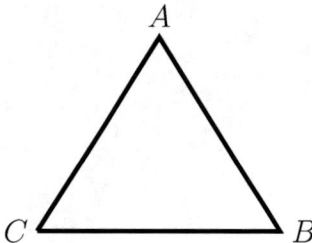

## Grades 9-10

(1) Find the lowest multiple of 7 such that dividing it by any of the numbers $2, 3, 4, 5,$ and $6$ yields a remainder of 1.

(2) Two different numbers $x$ and $y$, not necessarily integers, satisfy the equation $x^3 - 1870x = y^3 - 1870y$. Find the value of $x^2 + xy + y^2$.

(3) Two riders on horseback simultaneously leave Village A. They proceed with different but constant speeds to Village B and then return without stopping. On her way back to Village A, one of the riders overtakes the other, meeting her at a point located $m$ miles from Village B. Upon returning to Village A, she leaves for Village B again and again meets the other rider after covering one third of the distance between Village A and Village B. Find the distance between the two villages.

## Grades 11-12

(1) When divided by 3, 6, and 12, a number has remainders $R_1$, $R_2$, and $R_3$, respectively. If the sum of the three remainders is equal to 15, what is $R_1$?

(2) A trapezoid $ABCD$, where $AB$ is parallel to $CD$, is circumscribed around a circle. The sides $AD$ and $BC$ are the diameters of two circles (not shown). Prove that these two circles are tangent, i.e. intersect at exactly one point.

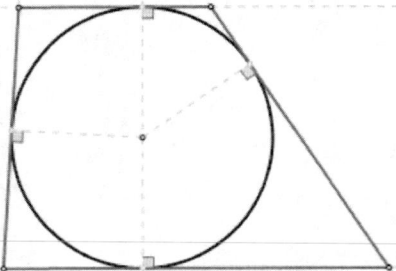

(3) Prove that there does not exist a continuous function $f(x)$ defined for all $x > 0$ such that $f(x)$ is rational if and only if $f(2x)$ is irrational.

## 2. Answers

**Grades 3-4**

(1) $C$

(2) North

(3) 2100 square centimeters

**Grades 5-6**

(1) 42

(2) $\dfrac{5}{8}$

(3) 2018

**Grades 7-8**

(1) 12

(2) STEVENS = 1930321 and HOBOKEN = 7565432. Therefore, HENS = 7321.

(3) $\dfrac{1}{8}$

**Grades 9-10**

(1) 301

(2) 1870 (this is the year in which Stevens was founded!)

(3) $6m$

**Grades 11-12**

(1) $R_1 = 1$. (The other remainders are $R_2 = 4$ and $R_3 = 10$. $R_2 - R_1$ is a multiple of 3, and $R_3 - R_2$ is a multiple of 6.)

(2) If a circle is inscribed in a quadrilateral, then the sums of the lengths of opposite sides are the same. The line connecting the centers of the tangent circles is the center line of the trapezoid and goes through the point of tangency. Its length is half the sum of the sides $AD$ and $BC$ and therefore equal to the sum of the radii of the two circles.

(3) Assume $f(x)$ is such a function, and consider the functions $g(x) = f(x) + f(2x)$ and $h(x) = f(x) - f(2x)$. Since the sum of a rational number and an irrational number is irrational, $g(x)$ and $h(x)$ take only irrational values and, since they are continuous, are therefore both constant. It follows that the function $g(x) + h(x) = 2f(x)$ is constant as well, which is a contradiction since it must have both rational and irrational values.

# SCAT Math Imitation Questions: Get Inspired by a 10-Year-Old

## Contents

(1) Foreword by Josephine Huang

(2) Foreword by Jake Wang

(3) Instructions

(4) 120 questions

(5) Answers

(6) About the Author

# SCAT Math Imitation Questions

## Grade level 4-7

(1) Foreword by Josephine Huang:

Challenge the Traditional Thematic Order

Jake is a ten-year-old fifth grader, studying at a public school in Niskayuna, New York. He shows great talent and high interest in math. He scores in the 99 percentile of the NWEA test. When he found us at Math is Fun Studio in Delmar, his math was already at $7^{th}$ grade level. We are thinking: What is the best way to teach Jake to turn math into a tool for thinking? We believe learning how to think creatively is a crucial thing in the age of Artificial Intelligence!

After quite some hard work, Jake made up all the SCAT imitation questions in this book all by himself! The amazing thing about this book is that Jake demonstrates a whole new way of learning math: It is not merely to be tested to see how much you understand math; it is to invent questions, to design your way of asking questions to reorganize what you have learned about math! By introducing Jake's book, we would like to invite all parents, teachers, and students to rethink what is learning in math!

There are many interesting designs you will discover in Jake's math questions. One of them I think is that he does not, deliberately, organize the sequence of questions into any thematic order. For example, in workbooks edited by grown-ups, you will have addition questions, then subtraction, then multiplication, and then division and fractions. Questions are classified in a thematic order. In Jake's book, you may be working on some fraction questions, and after a few other kinds of questions, you will encounter fractions again.

This is very interesting because thematic order in math workbooks creates the opportunity for one to gain familiarity through repetitive practicing. Repetitively practicing on the same math skill can sharpen that particular skill of solving. However, Jake's arrangement challenges that formation of familiarity. When you solve one question and feel that you are just about to get used to using the skill needed, you face a different type of question immediately. This might not be easy training for beginners. But it is a good training especially for one who is getting ready for an exam. You don't let your brain easily get too comfortable due to the repetitive appearance of a certain type of question. You train your brain to always get ready for being alert when reading questions, and when judging what skills you need to use. This interesting design in Jake's imitation questions is a fun exercise for students to practice getting ready for new challenges every time!

Enjoy the questions, enjoy the exercise! Maybe, you want to help your children or students make up their own imitation questions, too!

## (2) Foreword by Jake Wang

I have taken a long time to make this book, and I have a specific reason. These questions are not just made to be practiced for the SCAT, but as an inspiration for your question designing journey.

My way of creating and designing questions for this book was first thinking of two random answers, comparing them, and making questions for each of them. Another way I used was first deciding which is greater and less and making answers and questions for the inequalities. You don't have to use my way. You can create your own question designing steps and become a question designer!

A couple of challenges are hidden inside designing. A major challenge I faced was that when you go further, you start to run out of questions, right? Here are some ways to resolve it.

If you need to, you can take a break to refresh your memory and brain. Try to make different questions with different formats and principles, or make questions from operations that you have forgotten to use. You could use other books, such as your textbooks, homework, or extra math workbooks to find inspirations for your questions.

These questions have a wide range of operations, so that every single skill in math for 4-7 grade levels is covered. The questions are in a random order so that you could always do different questions and always review topics. *There are some tricky questions in the book to make sure that there is a sense for reading closely on some questions so that further mistakes on a future test are avoided.*

These questions are for both inspiration for making your own questions and preparation for the actual test.

Good luck!

Many thanks to my parents, Joyce Ni and Danny Wang. Thanks to Math is Fun Studio for initiating to publish this book!

## (3) Instructions for the test (Same as SCAT format)

This is what you will see at the SCAT and the Johns Hopkins CTY website.

Each question has two parts. The first part is in Column A. The second part is in Column B. You must decide if one part is greater than the other, if the two parts are equal, or if there is not enough information to decide. Then choose one of the following answers:

> A) The part in Column A is greater
>
> B) The part in column B is greater
>
> C) The two parts are equal
>
> D) Not enough information is given for you to decide

## (4) Questions

|   | Column A | Column B |
|---|---|---|
| 1 | $0.\overline{3}$ | $\dfrac{3}{9}$ |
| 2 | $\dfrac{4449}{1000}$ | $0.4449$ |
| 3 | $0.00000019$ | $0.0000000019$ |
| 4 | $0.103400009$ | $0.10340009$ |
| 5 | $\dfrac{1}{3}$ | $0.25$ |
| 6 | $0.\overline{35}$ | $\dfrac{35}{99}$ |
| 7 | $\dfrac{19}{7}$ | $2.45$ |

| 8 | $\dfrac{197}{346}$ | $\dfrac{394}{692}$ |
|---|---|---|
| 9 | $4 \times 10^{-3}$ | 0.0004 |
| 10 | 0.0000009 | 0.00001 |
| 11 | **Minutes in a hour** | **5 × 12** |
| 12 | Seconds in an hour | Degrees in a circle |
| 13 | The volume of a square pyramid with sides of 4 and height of 3 | 4 × 3 |

|    | Column A | Column B |
|----|----------|----------|
| 14 | $3x = 2x + 9$ $x = ?$ | $4x + 3 = 5x - (63 \div 9$ $x = ?$ |
| 15 | $\sqrt[3]{8}$ | $\sqrt[4]{16}$ |
| 16 | $\dfrac{125}{6} \times 0$ | $-7$ |
| 17 | The sum of the first 5 Fibonacci numbers | $|-13|$ |

| | Column A | Column B |
|---|---|---|
| 18 | The amount of zeroes in one decillion | $11 \times 3$ |
| 19 | The sides of a dodecagon | $3 \times 8 \div 2$ |
| | Column A | Column B |
| 20 | 2012022012 | 2022012012 |
| 21 | The days in three normal years (not leap) | Three times the sum of the days in January to July (not leap years) |
| 22 | $9^3$ | $5 \times 124$ |
| 23 | $2^3 \times 4 - 3^2$ | $2 \times (5 + 6)$ |

| | | |
|---|---|---|
| 24 | $7 \times 3 + 5$ | $7 \times 8 + 1$ |
| 25 | $16^2 \times 2$ | $2^{10} - 513$ |
| 26 | $200^2$ | $3^{3^3}$ |
| 27 | The weeks in a year | $5 \times 11$ |
| 28 | The sides on a cube | $3 \times 2$ |
| 29 | The vertices on a cube | The faces on a dodecahedron |
| 30 | All possible combinations on a Rubik's 5x5 | All the possible combinations on a Rubik's Pyraminx |
| 31 | $8 \times 90$ | $9 \times 80$ |

|    | Column A | Column B |
|----|----------|----------|
| 32 | $27 \times 3$ | $10 \times 10$ |
| 33 | $3^2$ | $2^3$ |
| 34 | $4^2$ | $2^4$ |
| 35 | $3 \times 9$ | $2 \times 13$ |
| 36 | $12^2 \times 3$ | $21^2$ |
| 37 | $9^2$ | $3^6$ |
| 38 | $3 \times 9$ | $3^3$ |
| 39 | $4^3$ | $3^4$ |
| 40 | $7 \times 5$ | $4 \times 8$ |
| 41 | $2^3 + 7$ | $3^2 - 3$ |
| 42 | $2 \times 3 \times 4$ | $4 \times 2 \times 3$ |
| 43 | The days in a year | Degrees in a circle plus 5 |

| | | |
|---|---|---|
| 44 | The months in a year | $3 \times 4$ |
| 45 | $3^2$ | The area of a 3x3 grid |
| 46 | $9 \times 9 \times 3$ | $3^5$ |
| 47 | $(8^2) \times (8^2)$ | $8^4$ |
| 48 | $3^3 \times 3$ | $9^2$ |
| 49 | $2^6$ | $6^3$ |
| 50 | $19 \times 3 + 3$ | $2 \times 7 \times 2$ |
| 51 | -7+(-9) | (-9)-(-7) |
| 52 | 9(-5)+50 | 8(-5)+45 |
| 53 | -17+17 | [-19+(-3)]+30 |
| 54 | $\sqrt{16}$ | $4^2$ |

|    | Column A | Column B |
|----|----------|----------|
| 55 | 19 | $36 \div 2$ |
| 56 | $\dfrac{\sqrt{9}}{2} + 1.5$ | $\sqrt{25} - 1$ |
| 57 | 0.75 | $\dfrac{3}{4}$ |
| 58 | Compare the quantity of numbers in the following number sequences for 58 and 59 | |
|    | 8,9,10,11…90,91 | 2,4,6,8,10…64,66 |
| 59 | 3,6,9,12…117,120 | 147,144,141…39 |

| 60 | 5! | 5 × 24 |
|---|---|---|
| 62 | $\dfrac{(19 \times 5 + 5)}{20}$ | $\sqrt{49}$ |
| 63 | 264+366 | $3^5$ |
| 64 | $\dfrac{8}{10}$ | $\dfrac{7}{8}$ |
| 65 | $\dfrac{5}{9}$ | $\dfrac{6}{10}$ |
| 66 | 3 Gallons | 11 Quarts |
| 67 | 3°C | 31°F |
| 68 | 400 × 100 ÷ 2 | 100 × 200 |
| 69 | $0.\overline{3} + \dfrac{1}{3}$ | 5 ÷ 6 |

| | | |
|---|---|---|
| 70 | $19 \times 20 + (29 - 10)$ | $2^9$ |
| 71 | 1 qumdecillion | 1 quarthor-decillion |
| 72 | $\infty^2$ | $\infty + \infty$ |
| 73 | 1 vigintillion | 1 novemdecillion |
| 74 | The zeroes in 1 centillion | $100 \times 3$ |
| 75 | 1+2+3+4…+100 | 5000 |
| 76 | 14 Gallons | 51 Quarts |

| | | |
|---|---|---|
| 77 | $10^5$ | $100^3$ |
| 78 | $10^{100}$ | Googol |
| 79 | $3 \uparrow 3$ | $3^{3^3} + 1$ |
| 80 | $\sqrt[3]{256}$ | $16^2$ |
| 81 | $121 \div 11 \div 11$ | $\sqrt{4}$ |
| 82 | $2^{10}$ | $4^5 + 3$ |
| 83 | $256 \times 4$ | $1000$ |
| 84 | $999^2 \times 0.\overline{373} \times 0$ | $i^4$ |

|    | Column A | Column B |
|----|----------|----------|
| 85 | The days in three normal years | The degrees in three circles + $\dfrac{45}{3}$ |
| 86 | The sides in a dodecagon and heptagon | The sides on two decagons |
| 87 | $2x(x+3)$ | $5x(x-7)$ |
| 88 | The volume of a cube 12 inches on each side | $12^3$ |

| | | |
|---|---|---|
| 89 | The volume of a sphere with a radius of 3 | 113 |
| 90 | The edges of three cubes | The total sides of a heptagon, nonagon, and decagon |
| 91 | 19=3n | 18+3n |
| 92 | $m \times 11 = 2$ | 0 |
| 93 | $\dfrac{14}{3} \times \dfrac{27}{7}$ | $5 \times 5 - 5$ |
| 94 | $\dfrac{7}{3}$ | $\dfrac{10}{5}$ |

| 95 | Sum of first three prime numbers | Sum of first three Fibonacci numbers |
|---|---|---|
| 96 | $27000 \div 9$ | $24000 \div 8$ |
| 97 | The average of the following: 1,9,7,4,5,3,1,2 | $\sqrt[3]{64}$ |
| 98 | The largest prime number above 119 | The largest prime number above 121 |
| 99 | The feet in 4 miles | The meters in 4 kilometers |
| 100 | $5^4$ | $25^2$ |

|     | Column A | Column B |
| --- | --- | --- |
| **101** | 19191191 | 19191919 |
| **102** | 20000+1993 | 1998+20005 |
| **103** | $10^{10^{100}}$ | googolplex |
| **104** | 0.0000991 | 0.000413 |
| **105** | The zeroes in a googolplex | googol |
| **106** | $\sqrt{17} \times 2 \times \sqrt{17}$ | $7 \times 5$ |
| **107** | $\sqrt{3} \times 3$ | $\sqrt{3} \times \sqrt{3}$ |
| **108** | The seconds in 24 hours | 86,200 |

| | | |
|---|---|---|
| 109 | The total seconds in 1 normal year | 41,538,000 |
| 110 | $2^{10}$ | $3^6$ |
| 111 | $2^{20}$ | $2^{10} \times 2$ |
| 112 | Round to the nearest one for questions 112-3 $(11 \times 19) \div 17$ | $10 \times \sqrt{5}$ |
| 113 | $\dfrac{23 \times 19}{5}$ | $9^2$ |
| 114 | $\left(\dfrac{19 \times 5}{5}\right)^2$ | $(20^2 + 19) - 27$ |
| 115 | $-\lvert-17\rvert \times 10^4$ | 0.0017 |
| 116 | $\dfrac{21}{15} \times \dfrac{10}{14}$ | $i^4$ |
| 117 | $\sqrt{3} \times 286 \times \pi \times 0$ | $-\lvert-396\rvert$ |
| 118 | $35 \times 50$ | $(35 \times 5)(35 \times 10)$ |
| 119 | $10!$ | $5! \times 2$ |
| 120 | $20!$ | $40! \div 2$ |

(5) Answers

1:C  2:A  3:A  4:B  5:A

6:C  7:A  8:C  9:A  10:B

11:C  12:A  13:B  14:B  15:C

16:A  17:B  18:C  19:C  20:B

21:A  22:A  23:A  24:B  25:A

26:A  27:B  28:C  29:B  30:A

31:C  32:B  33:A  34:C  35:A

36:B  37:B  38:C  39:B  40:A

41:A  42:C

43:D ( The question didn't specify if it was a leap year or not)

44:C  45:C

46:C  47:C  48:C  49:B  50:A

51:B  52:C  53:B  54:B  55:B

56:B    57:C    58:A    59:A    60:C

61:B    62:B    63:B    64:B    65:B

66:A    67:A    68:C    69:B    70:B

71:A (qumdecillion is 1 followed by 48 zeroes and quarthordecillion is 1 followed by 45 zeroes)

72:C

73:A (vigintillion is 1 followed by 63 zeroes and novemdecillion is 1 followed by 60 zeroes)

74:A (centillion is 1 followed by 303 zeroes)

75:A

76: A  77: B  78:C

79: B (3 up-arrow 3 is 3 cubed cubed, or 48,643)

80:B    81:B    82:B    83:A

84:B ( "i" is the square root of -1, so "i" to the fourth power is 1)

85:C

86:B 87:D 88:C 89:A 90:A

91:B 92:A 93:A 94:A 95:A

96:C 97:C 98:C 99:A 100:C

101:B 102:B 103:C 104:B 105:C

106:B 107:A 108:A 109:B 110:A

111:A 112:B 113:A 114:B 115:B

116:C 117:A 118:A 119:A 120:B

# About the Author, Jake Wang

Jake Wang

5th Grade Craig Elementary School, Niskayuna, New York

Why I love Math?

Math is my favorite subject, and I like it because in math, you can't just memorize math, you have to work it out. I developed a childhood interest in math when I was little, and it turned out to be really helpful in school.

There are many subjects and concepts in math, and that's what makes it fun, and I hope you love math, too!

If you study hard enough and practice your facts, there will be lots of good things waiting for you in the future, trust me, hard work *always* pays off!

When I was little, my mom would always teach me concepts in math. She would teach me things like pairs of ten, or addition, and by first grade, I had mastered the times table, one row at a time. I am very thankful for my mom helping me on this journey.

I think math is important. One day, when I was in fourth grade, one of my teachers brought in a sheet of paper to our class listing many jobs that included or used math. In my spare time, I looked at that paper and studied many of the jobs listed. I couldn't think of a job not listed on the sheet, meaning that math was used almost everywhere.

I also think math is crucial because of my early learning experience with my mom at home: I had discovered that there are many mysteries to think about in math. Math is not boring at all. I learned math everywhere, everyday.

Published by Math is Fun Studio, 2017
Copyright belongs to Jake Wang

Made in the USA
Middletown, DE
15 April 2018